Looking Ahead:

Identifying Key Economic Issues for Business and Society in the 1980s

The Heffernan Press Inc., Worcester, Massachusetts
Design: Stead, Young & Rowe Inc.

Library of Congress Cataloging in Publication Data

Schiff, Frank W
  Looking ahead.

    1.   United States—Economic conditions—1971-
2.   United States—Economic policy—1971-
3.   Economic forecasting—United States.   I.   Committee
for Economic Development.   II.   Title.
HC106.7.S34   338.973   80-27248
ISBN 0-87186-333-2 (pbk.)

First printing: December 1980
Paperbound: $5.00

COMMITTEE FOR ECONOMIC DEVELOPMENT
477 Madison Avenue, New York, N.Y. 10022
1700 K Street, N.W., Washington, D.C. 20006

Looking Ahead:

Identifying Key
Economic Issues
for Business
and Society
in the 1980s

Prepared by
Frank W. Schiff

Committee for
Economic Development

CED RESEARCH ADVISORY BOARD

CONTENTS

FOREWORD

In an era of rapid change and great uncertainty, it is a formidable challenge to anticipate problems and identify issues that will be crucial for the national economy in the years ahead. *Looking Ahead: Identifying Key Economic Issues for Business and Society in the 1980s* is the product of CED's effort to foresee a number of the large and complex forces and problems in our economic future and to provide a framework within which effective policy decisions can be made.

This Research Memorandum was conceived as a means of helping the CED Research and Policy Committee plan its future program of studies. Discussions with CED Trustees, other business leaders, and academic experts over a two-year period identified an agenda of key economic issues: those that are likely to exert a strong influence on business and society in the 1980s. So great was the interest in these crucial issues, both inside and outside CED, that this publication is being distributed widely to business, government, educational and research institutions, and foundations for use as a reference in sorting out the problems that deserve serious attention in this decade.

Two main information-gathering techniques were used in formulating the list of issues: personal interviews and round-table discussions involving varying proportions of senior corporate executives and professional economists. In each case, discussants were provided with a summary of the ideas generated at previous meetings so that there was a progressive refinement of focus on the various topics.

This report does not attempt to present detailed analyses or policy recommendations on the problems identified as key issues. Nor does it attempt to rank these issues in order of importance. Indeed, there may be honest differences about what constitutes a key issue and how it should be defined. The paper simply identifies those economic problems that a group of knowledgeable business leaders, in discussions with staff and academic experts, have regarded as most worthy of attention and consideration in the decade ahead. It clearly represents a *business perspective* on these problems, albeit one informed and conditioned by scholarly advice. As such, it can be useful to those striving to understand which major economic issues need to be better researched, understood, and dealt with.

I wish to acknowledge the valuable assistance we received from CED Trustees and other national business leaders, from CED's advisors, and from others in business, academic, and research institutions who helped us to identify and clarify the various issues described in this volume. It was Frank W. Schiff, CED's Vice President and Chief Economist, to whom we turned, once the list of issues was compiled and classified, to develop the summary description and analysis of each issue. I want to thank him personally for the thought-stirring way in which he developed, with the benefit of comments from Trustees, advisors, and other staff members, each issue in this document. I believe that our primary objective of being helpful and stimulative to those engaged in the process of determining what practical economic problems to study is well served by this report.

The Committee for Economic Development is indebted to the Exxon Education Foundation for its generous support of this project.

Robert C. Holland
President
Committee for Economic Development

1.
INTRODUCTION

The issues presented in this publication have been separated into two distinct groups: those representing *fundamental forces* that, as a practical matter, cannot be halted and that therefore need to be taken into account in any policy planning and those constituting *problem areas* that can be addressed and resolved, at least in part, through proper decisions and that need timely policy attention. These issues are regarded as needing serious attention by policy makers during the next five to ten years. Some are expected to grow significantly in importance in future years; others are already of very serious dimensions and are expected to remain so for at least much of the 1980s.

Among the *fundamental forces* is the complex of demographic and labor force changes: the aging of the postwar baby-boom generation, the rise in the number of the elderly, the increase in labor force participation of women, the growing number of Spanish-speaking workers, and the prospect of shortages in the supply of some types of skills. The sheer magnitude of such changes is deemed great enough to alter American society and to call for fundamental changes in its major institutions.

Another force cited is the increasing economic interdependence of nations. Recent events have highlighted the extent to which inflation and recession can spread across national borders and the rapidity with which supply shocks related to energy and food, for example, can exert cumulative effects throughout the world economic system. Economic policies in a wide variety of fields formerly regarded as purely domestic can be expected to exert an increasingly significant influence on economic developments in other countries and on their industrial policies.

Among the *problem areas* that need priority attention are three unusually pervasive issues: inflation, taxes, and the ability to adjust to economic change. Inflation is recognized as a problem that can inflict severe damage on the institutions that bind this society together. The report highlights the most significant issues surrounding future policies to combat inflation: the use of fiscal and monetary policies, supply-side policies aimed at increasing productive capacity and productivity, measures to strengthen investment in physical and human capital, the role of restrictive economic policies and government regulations, efforts to reduce the economy's vulnerability to shocks, and alternative means of exerting influence on wage and price decisions. The challenge will be to find ways of curbing inflation while promoting longer-term economic growth and high employment.

Public hostility toward the tax structure, whether at the federal, state, or local level, is likely to intensify in the coming decade. Proposals for reform will be aimed at making the tax system both more equitable and less complex. The role of taxation is a vital factor in furthering economic performance. Therefore, a critical issue will be how to change the system to provide more incentives, and to reduce disincentives, for saving, investment, and risk taking and to shift to greater relative reliance on taxes that fall on consumption.

The ability to adjust to economic change is crucial to a dynamic and productive economy. Asking the right questions about the appropriate role of government in assisting this process may be as important as finding immediate answers. Many of these questions relate to issues that are often combined under the general heading of "industrial policy," though they can also be considered under separate headings, as is done later in this study.

Among the questions that need to be asked are the following: Should public policies mainly rely on general measures that will create a sound environment for growth in all industries and regions, such as steps to strengthen the competitive market system and to encourage more investment and innovation? To what extent should public policies be more specifically geared to assisting growth and adjustment in particular sectors, industries, and regions? Should such assistance mainly involve such steps as removal of unnecessary regulations and assurance of fair treatment for the products of these industries under international trading rules? Or should there be more active assistance to particular industries, perhaps even involving government efforts to pick likely winners in domestic and international economic competition?

At the other end of the spectrum, what (if anything) should be done to aid the losers? Should the government provide assistance to those adversely affected by change only if the change that produced the damage is the direct result of government action? To what extent should assistance focus on individuals, businesses, communities? How much can be accomplished by such readjustment measures as retraining and relocation? Should there be direct compensation in cases in which readjustment is impossible?

Many of the problems identified in this report are often exacerbated by a sense of antagonism between government and business. A challenge in the coming decade will be to clarify the optimal role of the private enterprise system, especially the corporation, in the economy and in society at large and to develop a clear understanding of that role by the general public. The report identifies opportunities for reducing the tension between business and government through broadening the scope of public-private partnerships in such areas as revitalizing America's cities, providing training and jobs for the hard-to-employ, improving educational services, and fostering increased energy production and conservation.

Other problem areas examined range from the need to adapt work patterns to changing societal requirements and attitudes to the need for developing better mechanisms for coordinating international economic policies. The objective of the report is, not to provide a list that embraces every conceivable economic issue demanding attention in the next decade, but to identify those relatively few areas in which solutions can make a crucial difference to the nation's future.

There are two unifying themes in this report. One is that the nation is losing its industrial preeminence and, consequently, its ability to compete successfully in many world markets. There was a strong feeling among those who participated in this project that the competitive vigor of the U.S. economy is a major factor in controlling inflation, providing adequate job opportunities, and achieving a healthy economy and a secure society.

Through most of modern history, the United States has led all other nations in the ability to produce efficiently, to grow, to innovate, to assure adequate services for a large and diverse population. But it has become all too clear that the country is losing that competitive edge. In the past decade, the United States has had a lower rate of increase in productivity than most of the major industrialized nations. Moreover, the United States is lagging behind its principal industrial competitors in the share of gross national product devoted to capital investment, saving, and research and development.

This memorandum deals directly with the issues that strongly influence the nation's competitive strength and vitality: the willingness to save and invest, to remove regulations that unduly stifle competition, to stimulate technological progress, and to increase productivity. Moreover, it reflects a view held with deep conviction by business leaders: namely, that restoring a highly productive, competitive, and noninflationary economy is fundamental to solving most of the other challenges the country faces, including assurance of adequate strength in national security and foreign policy and attainment of key domestic social and economic goals, ranging from revitalization of the cities to a cleaner environment, quality education, and greater security in old age.

The second unifying theme, which is closely related to the first, is that the entire process of governance is in need of repair and modernization. On many key issues, it currently does not seem possible to form the coalitions and develop the consensus necessary to produce positive political decisions. "The process," said one participant in our discussions, "has broken down."

To be sure, it is easy, in the midst of our current frustrations, to underestimate past difficulties with the governing process. Nonetheless, the net impression of the participants was that the capacity to reach consensus has degenerated. Many see the current proliferation of relatively well-organized and uncompromising single-interest forces at the root of the present difficulties. Our society has increasingly been unable to produce a comprehensive economic policy that meets national needs and is at the same time reasonably acceptable to divergent interests.

The influences contributing to this impasse are many and varied. Our present-day problems are far more complex and interrelated, so much so that we cannot simply go back to procedures that were effective in the past. Our institutions have often failed to keep pace with basic technological, economic, and societal changes. There is a wide range of conflicts among various groups in our society and among different sectors and regions. We distrust one another. In an era in which our available resources do not match our expectations, we seem unwilling to lower our sights where necessary, to limit our claims, to sacrifice in the larger interest. The result has been that it is often far easier for special interests to prevent needed actions than it is to achieve broad agreement on solutions that reflect common interests and shared objectives.

The challenge implicit in these themes is a formidable one: to rebuild a more cohesive society, with better economic policies serving an accepted set of broad societal goals. One essential ingredient for meeting that challenge is greater understanding on the part of a more enlightened public. This report seeks to encourage the kind of understanding that will enable the leaders of the nation's institutions to set priorities and forge a consensus on the crucial economic issues that will confront business and society in the coming decade.

2. FUNDAMENTAL FORCES

This chapter offers a brief discussion of the fundamental forces that are expected to have major effects on the economy in the 1980s and beyond and that need to be given special consideration by policy makers.

Demographic and Labor Force Changes. In the 1980s, a much larger proportion of the population and the work force than in the 1970s will be in the prime-age category (twenty-five to forty-four), reflecting the aging of the postwar baby-boom generation. At the same time, the relative overall importance of teen-agers and young adults as a segment of the labor force will decline. Other significant trends include a continued increase in the labor force participation of women (some forecasters predict that by 1990, the female participation rate will have risen as much as 10 percentage points above the 51 percent rate recorded in early 1979); a further rise, though at a declining rate, in the population share of persons who are 65 or older; and according to official projections, a continued downward trend in the labor force participation rate of persons who are 55 and over. The last-mentioned projection is, however, subject to special uncertainties. It assumes continuation of the trend toward earlier retirement, a tendency that might well be reversed as a result of inflationary pressures, the increase in the permissible mandatory retirement age to 70, and the development of more part-time jobs and other flexible work opportunities.

In general, current trends suggest that the coming decade's labor force is likely to be more stable and potentially more productive than the labor force of the 1970s. This view is based primarily on the observation that the prime-age groups, which will be of such importance in the 1980s, have customarily been more regular participants in the labor market than other groups and contain a high percentage of persons with considerable training and experience. On average, moreover, the work force in the 1980s will be substantially better educated than it has been in the past, although the evidence of major educational deficiencies and the appallingly high dropout rates in some areas make it clear that the average numbers mask major shortcomings in the education of some groups, notably minorities and others who are disadvantaged. The prospective changes in labor force composition may make it easier to achieve somewhat lower overall unemployment rates with given levels of capacity utilization and rates of economic expansion than was possible in prior years.

However, there are also potential sources of difficulties. As relatively fewer youths enter the labor force, shortages in the supply of workers for skilled entry-level positions may emerge, as already appears to be the case in engineering. At the same time, competition among prime-age workers for middle-level jobs is likely to become more intense, and there will be reduced opportunities for rapid advancement to higher positions. Demographic trends will not necessarily help to reduce the disproportionately high unemployment among blacks and other minority groups because (in contrast with the trend for whites) the percentage of nonwhite teen-agers and young adults in the labor force will show little (if any) decline.

Changes in the Nonworker/Worker Ratio. A key influence on productivity, living standards, social security burdens, and the degree of economic conflict will be the so-called economic dependency ratio, that is, the ratio of nonworkers to workers in the total population.

The demographic factors described in the preceding section suggest that this ratio may actually decline over the next decade, so that those who work would support fewer nonworkers than before. However, institutional and attitudinal factors could change this result. Thus, some experts believe that such developments as increased length of schooling, a trend toward earlier retirement, and pressures for a shorter workweek and fewer workdays per year for full-time workers could lead to a rise in the ratio over the coming decade. But this view, too, is open to challenge, partly because of uncertainties regarding retirement age trends and partly because of potential increases in the volume of part-time work.

In any case, it is likely that the dependency ratio will rise again early in the next century. Although the proportion of young dependents in the population will be declining, there will be a sharp increase in both the absolute number and the population share of older persons. Starting in about 2010, as the baby-boom generation begins to reach retirement age, we can expect a dramatic rise in the ratio of retired to active workers and in the economic burden that this will impose on the working population, assuming no major changes in currently projected trends in labor force participation and retirement patterns. Because of the importance of adequate advance planning in such areas as social security and pension design, these prospective developments after the turn of the century could thus be a crucial consideration in connection with decisions that need to be made during the 1980s.

Changing Character of Work. The nature of work will continue to change as the United States becomes more and more dependent on professional, technical, and clerical skills, rather than on muscle power. Over 60 percent of employment is now attributable to service industries. In 1979, 51 percent of the work force was classified as white collar and only 33 percent as manual or blue collar, with more than 25 percent consisting of professionals and managers. The trend toward technical and service-type jobs, especially in information-related fields, is expected to continue or even accelerate in the decade ahead.

Continued rapid advances in technology, particularly in the computer field, will have a major impact on the nature of a wide range of jobs, with increasing numbers of people relying on computers in some phase of their activities. The character of office work, for example, may well be changed drastically by the application of the new technology. It is also likely that the nature of work will be affected by growing worker and employer interest in the further "humanizing" of the workplace, which involves more systematic efforts to redesign jobs and effect other improvements in the quality of work life. Many of the prospective changes in the nature of work can be expected to emerge as a result of new attitudes toward work on the part of many young people and as responses to the needs of the growing number of women, minorities, and older people in the work force. All this should produce increasing emphasis on more flexible arrangements with respect to work time and even the place of work and on wider use of part-time work arrangements, including such innovative techniques as job sharing.

A New Public Questioning of Economic Decisions. Both business and government face a growing number of challenges concerning the fairness and reasonableness of their economic actions, and this development is expected to be a major force impinging on the decisions of policy makers in the years ahead.

In the private sector, a whole range of management decisions is now subject to much greater questioning by workers, consumers, and community groups, either directly or through their government representatives. Hiring, firing, job assignments, plant location, plant closings, product design, and the introduction or termination of a service or product line are some of the more noteworthy areas in which prerogatives that formerly belonged to management are now effectively constrained by others through objections, demonstrations, or resort to litigation or new legislation.

At the government level, Proposition 13, campaigns for constitutional amendments to limit government spending, and protests over energy policy and nuclear safety are symptomatic of a growing public willingness to challenge established ways of dealing with economic problems. Given rapid inflation as well as heavier tax burdens, such questioning should become even more insistent, particularly on the part of those who believe that the middle class is receiving especially unfair treatment. Public restiveness over economic decisions is likely to be aggravated by the realization that many experts who participate in the making of economic policies are themselves far less certain than they have been in the past about what constitutes the right kind of policies.

Growing International Interdependence. The dramatic growth in international interdependence that characterized the 1970s can be expected to continue, spurred in part by further advances in communication and transportation and by the increasing integration of world financial markets. Such integration gives borrowers in individual countries access to a much wider range of financing sources and at the same time sharply reduces the scope for independent national monetary policy actions. As was stated in a recent study by the Joint Economic Committee of Congress, "Goods, money, people, ideas, and problems are traveling across national boundaries as never before."[1] Recent events have highlighted the extent to which inflation and recession can spread across national borders and the rapidity with which supply shocks related to energy and food can exert cumulative effects throughout the world economic system. Moreover, economic policies in a wide variety of areas once regarded as purely domestic can be expected to exert an increasingly significant influence on eco-

[1]Alfred Reifman, *The U.S. Role in a Changing World Economy* (Joint Economic Committee Print, June 25, 1979).

nomic developments in other countries, including, for example, national industrial policies.

Increasing Importance of Developing Countries. The 1980s should witness a further significant rise in the relative political and economic power of the developing countries. In part, this will stem from the greater influence of the oil-producing nations and the enormous increase in the volume of capital funds at their disposal. In part, it reflects the rising importance of the growing (although still limited) number of developing countries that are becoming more fully industrialized (e.g., Brazil, Mexico, Korea, and Taiwan). Some of these countries are already important exporters of a wide range of manufactured goods, including electronic and other engineering products. At the same time, these and other developing nations are becoming much more important markets for the manufactured products of the developed world. The likely rise in the importance of developing countries, even the poorest ones, will be enhanced by their rapidly growing influence in the international political arena and in international organizations and lending institutions. For some of the non-oil-producing developing nations, however, these favorable prospects could be thwarted if balance-of-payments and financial difficulties should force them into severe retrenchment.

Inflation, Taxes, and a Changing Economy

Better Policies for Curtailing Inflation. The escalation of inflation after successive periods of economic slack is raising basic questions about our society's ability to overcome this pernicious addiction. The damage inflation does to the fabric of both our economic system and our society is so great that it must not be allowed to proceed unchecked. A crucial challenge over the next few years will be to make determined progress toward resolving this problem in ways that are conducive to longer-term economic growth and high employment.

If the challenge is to be met, key questions must be answered: How can existing approaches to the use of fiscal and monetary policies and targets be improved? How can greater and more effective use be made of supply-oriented policies aimed at increasing productive capacity and productivity, particularly measures designed to strengthen investment in physical and human capital? What policies are needed to reduce restrictive economic practices and regulations and thereby give increased scope to free market mechanisms? What can be done to decrease the vulnerability of the economy to external and other shocks? To what extent can the problem be mitigated by greater use of cost-containment efforts in specialized areas, such as medical care? What are the pros and cons of alternative means of exerting more direct influence on wage and price decisions? In this connection, what role (if any) should be played by new techniques for resolving labor-management conflicts, by voluntary or compulsory wage-price guidelines, and by the use of tax incentives or disincentives to induce more moderate wage and price behavior?

Reforming the Tax Structure. The existing widespread dissatisfaction with many aspects of the present tax structure at the federal, state, and local levels is likely to become even more intense in the coming decade. Proposals for reform will aim at making the system more conducive to efficient economic performance, more equitable, and less complex. An important part of the debate will focus on the relative priorities that should be assigned to these and other goals and on how and to what extent conflicts among various goals can best be resolved.

From the point of view of encouraging higher levels of economic output and productivity, the key issue will be how to change the system in order to provide more incentives (and to reduce disincentives) for saving, investment, and risk taking and in order to shift to greater relative reliance on taxes that fall on consumption. Central questions of tax equity will be whether more regular and frequent adjustments in the tax structure should be made to offset inflation-induced increases in the real tax burden and whether ways can be found to offset the regressive aspects of successive increases in social security taxes. Other questions will relate to the relative desirability of across-the-board tax adjustments (such as general reductions in corporate or personal income taxes) and of selective tax measures targeted to particular activities and objectives (such as the investment tax credit and employment tax credits for hiring the hard-to-employ). Even more fundamentally, major questions are likely to be raised regarding the overall level of taxation, its impact on particular groups (notably the middle class), and the relative extent to which government at all levels should rely on expenditures, tax provisions, and regulations to achieve public objectives.

Adjusting for the Adverse Effects of Inflation. As overall inflation has mounted, more groups and institutions have attempted to find ways to protect themselves from its effects. The rapid recent spread of formal and informal indexation arrangements is likely to continue in the years immediately ahead. Public policy has, in fact, tended to encourage this trend. Thus, at the present time, nearly 60 percent of the federal budget is directly or indirectly subject to some form of indexation to the price level. Should indexation be further encouraged in the coming years, or should it be resisted on the ground that such adjustments are likely to be major contributors to a continuing inflationary spiral? Can rational ways be found to distinguish between desirable and undesirable types of inflation adjustments?

Adjusting to the Adverse Effects of Economic Change. If the U.S. economy is to be dynamic and productive in the 1980s, it must be able to respond flexibly to a wide range of changes. Many of these will benefit a majority of the population but may nevertheless impose relatively serious hardships on particular individuals, firms, industries, or communities. The question of how to deal with the adverse effects of economic change is likely to arise in numerous contexts: for example, in connection with the impact of changing trade and investment patterns, shifts in the economic importance of different regions of the country, the employment and locational impact of technological innovations and productivity increases, changes in environmental standards and other regulatory requirements, and increased stress on free market pricing and deregulation. In many cases, development of better ways to adjust to economic change will be desirable not only to cope with changes that have already occurred but also to permit needed structural improvements that would be successfully resisted in the absence of adequate provisions to deal with potential losers.

In designing more effective means of adjusting to change, numerous issues will have to be faced. Is it preferable to deal with different types of adjustment on an ad hoc basis, or can a generalized approach be evolved? Should government assistance be provided only if the change that produced the damage is the direct result of government action? To what extent should assistance focus on individuals, on business firms, or on communities? How much can or should be accomplished by early identification of emerging difficulties; by positive steps to respond to change, such as retraining and relocation; or by direct compensation in cases where readjustment is not possible?

The Public
Policy Process

Sharpening Fiscal Control. In the face of continued inflationary burdens, taxpayer revolts, pressures for large new spending programs (e.g., for defense and medical care), and simultaneous public dissatisfaction with the performance of many existing government programs, the issue of sharpening methods of fiscal control is likely to move to the center of public debate. People are asking increasingly tough questions about the need for various types of public programs and the effectiveness with which tax dollars are being spent. As a consequence, continued stress will be placed on possible improvements in the congressional and executive budget processes, including improved controls over government credit activities. At the state and local levels, the need for greatly improved management and financial accountability will be highlighted.

The accompanying public debate should focus attention on two broadly distinguishable approaches: On the one hand, how much can be accomplished by improved methods of evaluating the costs and benefits of government spending, by stepped-up efforts to increase government productivity, and by such techniques as multiyear budgeting and basic reappraisals of major programs to take them out of the "uncontrollables" category? On the other hand, what are the relative advantages and disadvantages of constitutional or legal limits on taxes and/or expenditures at the federal, state, and local levels, and what is the potential role of sunset legislation?

Fundamentally, of course, the need is to face up frankly to budget priorities and, even more broadly, to the way in which the nation sh ould allocate its total resources, both public and private. Of y importance in this connection will be the assessment of future defense spending needs and the methods chosen to finance such spending. If, as is widely believed, a strong need exists for a major buildup in the U.S. defense capacity, effective ways must also be found to finance that buildup in a noninflationary fashion. Moreover, a broad view of national security requirements will call for hard decisions about the relative allocation of national resources to direct military spending, to building up capital investment and energy supply, and to social and other expenditures needed to preserve the underlying strength of our economy and society.

Improving the Federal Economic Policy Process. The federal government's performance has been sadly disappointing in many respects. Much of the fault lies in the way it makes and implements economic policy. If that performance is to be improved, several key questions must be answered: How can the federal government relate its near-term decisions more effectively to longer-range goals and results? What role can multiyear budgeting play in this connection? How can a similar longer-range perspective be developed for supply-related policies? How can the impact of individual economic policy actions on one another and on the full range of economic policy goals be more systematically analyzed and taken into account in actual decisions? How can systematic consideration of free market and incentive approaches be made an integral part of the policy process? What steps (if any) are needed to improve coordination of fiscal policies, monetary policies, and the activities of federal credit agencies? How can implementation of government programs that involve a multiplicity of government departments and agencies be effectively coordinated not only at the federal level but also at the regional and local levels, where such coordination is often even more important? How can efforts to improve government decision making and policy implementation be carried out in ways that do not add unnecessarily to bureaucracy, paper work, and confusion? Finally, what can be done to expedite the remedying of mistakes once they are discovered?

Reforming Government Regulation. Given the enormous increase in the extent, complexity, and cost of government regulation, pressure for reform can be expected to intensify over the next decade. Part of the debate is likely to focus on whether particular economic goals can be more effectively achieved through government intervention or through reliance on competitive market processes. In some areas, such as nuclear safety, there will be strong demands for a tightening of regulations. In many others, however, the central issue will be how to reduce the scope and rigidity of regulation and encourage a trend toward deregulation along the lines recently introduced in the airline industry. Even where some form of government involvement seems indicated, much more attention will probably be given to the form that such involvement should take.

Some of the particular questions that the issue of regulatory reform will raise are: What can be done to reduce the use of command-and-control-type regulations (those that involve government specifications regarding the methods by which desired results are to be achieved) and to place increased reliance on regulations that focus on performance results, leaving industry free to find the most efficient ways of achieving them? What can be done to improve measurement of the costs, benefits, and side effects of regulation? How can the overall design and management of the regulatory process be strengthened to make it speedier, more effective, and less inflationary? Can better procedures be established to resolve conflicts or set priorities in cases in which regulations have differential effects on major national objectives, such as those relating to price stability, energy, and the environment?

Better Coordination of International Economic Decision Making. Greatly increased international interdependence in a wide range of fields makes improved coordination of national economic policies an increasingly urgent issue. Coordination need not imply a move toward identical policies. Rather, it should involve increased cooperation in tackling common problems such as curtailing worldwide inflation, combating recession, and meeting energy and food needs. It also calls for greater concern with the impact that the actions of individual countries have on other countries and on common international goals. What is required to improve the mechanisms for such coordination? To what extent does the solution lie in clearer delineation of the functions of existing international organizations, such as the International Monetary Fund, the International Bank for Reconstruction and Development, the Organization for Economic Cooperation and Development, the General Agreement on Tariffs and Trade, and the United Nations? Can, and should, the role of economic summit meetings be regularized and strengthened? Should new international organizations or mechanisms for coordination be created? Is there a role that voluntary private-sector cooperation can play? What changes in existing codes of economic conduct are desirable, and in which areas (e.g., industrial policy) is there a need for developing new agreements? How can movements toward greater regional economic integration be reconciled with a more general harmonization of international economic policies? Is improved coordination possible not only among the major industrial countries but also between these countries and key oil-producing nations, other developing countries, and the Communist Bloc?

Coordinating Federal, State, and Local Policies. How federal policies designed to achieve national purposes in state and local jurisdictions can best be reconciled with local responsibility and initiative will continue to be a key issue. Should there be basic changes with respect to the level of government at which particular functions are carried out? What can be done to reduce the conflicts in applicable laws, regulations, and administrative practices among different levels of government? What other steps are needed to render policy making by government units at various levels complementary rather than competitive?

Better Use of the Private Sector in Government Policy Making. Many failures of government policy have resulted from an inadequate understanding of legitimate private-sector concerns and a failure to make effective use of the talents and resources of that sector (both profit and nonprofit). How can Congress and the executive branch make better use of constructive private-sector contributions and at the same time resist undue influence by private groups concerned with narrow self-interests? How can improved arrangements along these lines best be developed at the federal, state, and local levels? To what extent is it desirable to formalize such arrangements? What should be the role of nonprofit organizations that focus on broad public policy issues?

The Role of Business in Society

Clarifying the Corporation's Function in Society. Lack of a clear understanding of this issue by the general public can itself be harmful to effective functioning of the private enterprise system. A better appreciation of the unique contribution of a competitive, profit-oriented private enterprise system to economic growth and efficient economic performance is required. In addition, a clearer definition is needed of the full range of responsibilities that corporations should assume in direct connection with their exercise of these basic economic functions — for example, as employers, as users of resources, as influences on the environment, and as important members of local communities. Most difficult is the task of determining the desirable extent of private-sector involvement in efforts to cope with major social problems, such as poverty and urban blight. What is the limit to which such involvement can be stretched without interfering unduly with the corporation's basic economic functions or with functions that should more appropriately be assumed by government?

Broadening the Scope of Public-Private Cooperation. There is growing evidence that the effective solution of many social and economic problems calls for greater reliance on public-private cooperation rather than reliance on government alone, particularly at the local level. CED's policy statement *Jobs for the Hard-to-Employ: New Directions for a Public-Private Partnership* (1978) itself provided such evidence and has been an important catalyst for expanded public-private cooperation in providing training and jobs for the structurally unemployed. Scope for much wider use of this kind of cooperation exists not only in the field of employment but also in connection with broader efforts to spur local economic development and revitalize America's cities, improve educational services for all age groups, foster increased energy production and conservation, and provide more adequate services in numerous other areas. The following are among the issues to be considered: How can such efforts best be initiated? Are new organizational arrangements needed to mobilize effective and sustained support? What can be done through wider use of specialized intermediate organizations, financial incentives, and government contracts with private firms? What is an appropriate degree of accountability to build into such cooperative ventures?

Changing Corporate Governance. The changing American society has brought with it changes in the governance of American corporations. The economic environment has placed new pressures on the traditional managerial and directorial functions of assuring the firm's efficiency, competitiveness, and profitability. Questions have arisen as to whether corporate decisions are excessively focused on short-term goals, specifically on reported quarterly profits. In addition, increased stress has been placed on corporate ethics and the accountability of management to directors, shareholders, and the public. To date, responses in corporate governance have included increased management and director attention to these challenges, development of more corporate codes of conduct, an expanding volume of corporate reporting, appointment of more directors who are independent of management, and strengthening and protecting the role of internal and outside auditors and the audit committee of the board. Have these changes sufficed to maintain the corporation as a good performer? Has a suitable balance between short-run and long-run objectives been achieved? Are further changes needed to serve these purposes?

Another category of changes is being called for by some corporate critics who advocate the commitment of the corporation to specified social objectives. They call for corresponding changes in the choice of managers and directors in order to assure greater attention to such objectives (e.g., placing labor representatives, community-group leaders, or consumer advocates on boards of directors). Additional proposals involve vesting relatively greater authority in the board of directors, particularly in the outside directors. To what extent do these social concerns necessitate or justify alternatives in corporate governance? Do the benefits of such governance changes outweigh the costs? A broader question is: How can a governing board of directors organize itself to strike a suitable modern-day balance between such objectives as aftertax profits, preservation of the environment, a happy work force, and a stable host community?

Increased Demands for Employee Participation in Management Decisions. The greatly increased importance of service occupations, rapid technological changes that affect the nature of work, and the higher educational levels of many workers are among the factors stimulating increased employee demands to participate in decisions traditionally reserved for management alone. Many of these demands relate to the way in which operations are conducted and call for joint problem solving. Other demands for worker participation (far less widespread in the United States than in Europe) go much farther, extending to such matters as decisions to open or close plants, relocate employees, choose product lines, and undertake particular corporate investments. To what extent do these demands warrant changes in procedures and information flows? To what extent is some sharing of decision-making authority justified? What are the best methods of achieving those changes deemed wise?

Capital Investment and Economic Growth

Decapitalization of Certain Industries. The nature of this issue was forcefully summarized in a 1978 speech by Fletcher L. Byrom, Chairman of the Koppers Corporation and Chairman of the Board of Trustees of the Committee for Economic Development:

> The most devastating effect of these changes [e.g., tax laws that provide inadequate incentives to capital investment and innovation, unrealistic depreciation guidelines, and excessively burdensome regulatory structures] and of the institutionalized inflation that they produce and exacerbate is the progressive liquidation of the capital base of the nation's economic system. This is happening rapidly — and perhaps irreversibly — because of the high fixed costs of new physical capital; the long lead time needed to expand or modernize capacity, or to enter a new product area; outmoded accounting practices and taxing policies; and wholly unrealistic depreciation policies.
>
> What we wind up with is a very inadequate real return on investment. . . . In a number of industries, profitability is not high enough to justify investment in either expanded capacity or improved production efficiency. For starters, I can name steel, nonferrous metals, railroads and airlines, the utilities and probably paper. . . .

The alternative, already under discussion for some problems, is public subsidy, which stands well along the downhill road to nationalization of basic industries. And the death stroke will be administered by the declining competitiveness of some of these industries, not only in foreign markets, but against imports in our own domestic markets.

We have a high-wage, high-capital-cost economy. We can't continue to be internationally competitive or preserve our unique and central role in the interdependent global economy unless we sustain our comparative advantage in efficiency and productivity by use of economies of scale. Yes, productivity involves workers' skills and attitudes. But it also demands, especially in capital-intensive industries, an investment in research and development, and the application, through capital investment, of technological innovations that reduce unit costs and lead to the introduction of new and more efficient products and processes.

What needs to be done to restore sufficient incentives to spur private industrial activity in these areas?

Raising the Levels of Saving, Capital Investment, Technology, and Productivity. The need for greatly increased capital investment, technological progress, and productivity must be brought to the forefront of national concern. Moreover, such a shift in priorities must be translated into needed changes in a wide range of national policies. There is broad agreement that recent U.S. performance in these areas has been far from satisfactory. There has been no net growth in labor productivity in the nonfarm business sector in the past two years, compared with a 2.2 percent average rate of growth over the preceding seventeen years. The GNP percentage of total business expenditures for new plant and equipment has remained in the range of 9½ to 10½ percent for the past five years. Yet, several recent studies, including one sponsored by CED,[1] indicate that a rise to about 12 percent in the GNP share of business investment expenditures will be necessary to achieve a rate of capital formation over the next five to ten years that will be adequate to cope both with socially mandated expenditures and with the basic growth needs of the economy. To reach such a goal will require a significantly faster increase in business investment spending than in the GNP itself.

The CED policy statement *Stimulating Technological Progress* (1980) identifies various key policy measures that are needed to encourage more adequate capital investment and sharpen incentives for technological progress. The policy statements *Jobs for the Hard-to-Employ: New Directions for a Public-Private Partnership* (1978) and *Improving Management of the Public Work Force: The Challenge to State and Local Government* (1978) suggested important directions for increasing the productivity of human resources. However, these and other recent CED studies only begin to explore the relevant range of issues. In particular, it is vital to probe more deeply into the puzzle of lagging productivity and to search for needed solutions.

[1] Robert Lindsay, ed., *The Nation's Capital Needs: Three Studies,* A Supplementary Paper (New York: Committee for Economic Development, 1979).

Preserving and Improving the Capital Facilities of America's Cities. Recent evidence suggests that the fiscal pressures which have adversely affected many American cities and other localities are leading to serious neglect of needed maintenance and the consequent deterioration of physical facilities and to inadequate preparation for meeting future capital needs. Over time, such practices will become increasingly costly and could prove a serious impediment to urban economic development. What can be done to focus more systematic attention on this problem? What measures are most likely to produce needed corrective actions on a cost-effective basis?

Facing Up to Transitional and Long-Term Energy Problems. How the United States and the world economy as a whole can best adjust to the prospect of the gradual depletion of oil, gas, and ultimately, coal reserves will become an increasingly urgent concern during the next decade. Because of the very long lead times involved in developing and applying new or improved energy technologies, decisions about alternative energy strategies must generally be made far in advance of the time when they can become effective. Among the questions that must be answered in the next decade are the following: What should be the nature and magnitude of research and related efforts to develop potential renewable energy sources such as solar and fusion energy? Given the fact that these or other new energy technologies are not likely to become predominant sources of energy supply until sometime in the next century, what is the optimum strategy for dealing with energy supply and consumption in the meantime? To what extent should the national energy effort be focused on conservation, and to what extent should it emphasize more rapid development of existing and alternative domestic energy sources? To assist both energy conservation and energy supply, what can be done to assure optimum reliance on market incentives and the price system? To what extent will there be a need for special government actions, and what form should such actions take? What contingency preparations are needed to protect against possible major disruptions in energy availability? How strong an effort can, and should, be made to expand the use of coal and nuclear power? What can be done to overcome potential obstacles to such expansion that are related to environmental and safety hazards? What is the best approach to fostering commercial-scale production of synthetic fuels, including coal gasification and the extraction of liquid fuels from coal and oil shale?[2] Now that a program for the development of synthetic fuels has been adopted, what decisions regarding the contemplated second stage should be made by the middle or latter part of the 1980s?

Coping with Potential Supply and Capacity Bottlenecks. An effective approach to the problem of bottlenecks is vitally important both to avoiding or minimizing inflationary shocks and to preventing significant lags in overall output and productivity. Because of the long lead times typically involved in measures that affect future supply capabilities, early action is especially important.

[2] For CED's policy recommendations in this area, see *Helping Insure Our Energy Future: A Program for Developing Synthetic Fuel Plants Now* (1979).

Among the key measures to be considered are tax and other incentives to encourage more rapid capital investment in areas of potential bottlenecks (notably more adequate capital recovery allowances); changes in environmental and other regulatory provisions that unduly hamper production; development of alternative supply sources, as in the case of synthetic fuels; and skill training and related programs to cope with potential bottlenecks in human resources.

It is also essential to determine whether more systematic approaches to the problem of supply and capacity bottlenecks should be developed, or whether problems in this area can best be handled by ad hoc arrangements. For example, should new organizational arrangements be devised to better anticipate the emergence of structural supply imbalances? Should government assistance be used to overcome or break bottlenecks in particular cases? How much reliance (if any) should be placed on international commodity agreements or commodity stockpiles? What can be done to assure that proposed cures in this area do not prove worse than the disease?

Problems of Toxic Products and Wastes. The recent upsurge of concern over toxic wastes is a portent of debates that will characterize much of the 1980s. How can a more consistent and effective approach to this problem be developed? What standards should be set regarding the appropriate reduction of risk associated with chemical substances? To what extent and under what circumstances will there be a need for detailed government attention to the methods used to eliminate or reduce such risks? What can be done to put greater stress on actual performance, particularly through increased use of financial incentives to induce firms to achieve desired end results? How can society best deal with highly toxic waste products, particularly in the nuclear area? What cooperative international efforts are required?

Human Resources

Achieving Sustainable High Employment. A major goal of national economic policy has been the attainment of high employment so that all those who are willing and able to work will be able to find useful jobs at reasonable wages. Yet, achievement of this goal on a sustained basis has remained elusive. A principal obstacle has been the fact that expansion of overall demand to reduce total unemployment will at some point cause the economy to reach capacity limits and result in accelerated inflation. Indeed, in situations in which inflation has attained very serious forward momentum, as it currently has, a strong argument can be made for allowing the economy to run at less than capacity for some time to help brake the inflationary momentum.

A major longer-term issue is whether combating inflation requires continuing maintenance of a relatively high degree of economic slack and unemployment, or whether high employment and noninflationary economic growth can, and should, be achieved simultaneously. Among the more specific issues to consider in connection with these alternatives are the following: How much unemployment (if any) is compatible with the goal of high employment? How can the potential inflationary impact of demand expansion be mitigated by policies other than those related to employment (e.g., by measures to reduce wage and price rigidities, increase productivity, and ease bottlenecks)? How, and to what extent, can joblessness be reduced by direct measures to overcome structural unemployment, particularly as it affects the more disadvantaged groups in our society and the unusually high unemployment among youths and in inner cities? What role can improved education and skill training play in this connection? How can frictional unemployment be minimized by better job placement and other steps to improve the functioning of the labor market? How can the role of the private sector in coping with structural and frictional unemployment be enlarged?

The problem of dealing with unemployment in recessions raises additional issues. How can the impact of unemployment be mitigated by programs targeted to the groups and areas most severely affected? To what extent is work sharing a desirable alternative to recession layoffs? What general policy measures (such as easing of monetary policies, tax cuts, and expenditure programs) should be given priority in antirecession strategies?

Adapting Work Patterns to Changing Needs and Attitudes. Increasing emphasis is likely to be placed on adapting work to the needs of people throughout their lives, not just at particular times. Major issues will be how increased options can be created for greater flexibility in work time, work sites, and job design and how the time and energies of individuals can best be allocated among work, volunteer activities, and leisure. Many jobs are still tailored to the requirements of a male head of household who is the sole family income earner and who works from nine to five for five days each week. How can future work arrangements take greater account of the special needs of working women with children, older persons who want to work part time, and young people who spend part of the day in school? To what extent can the traditional division of lifetime careers into distinct periods of schooling, work, and retirement be modified to permit an intermingling of schooling and work throughout a person's active years, to place much greater emphasis on training for second careers, and to provide for a much more gradual transition to retirement?

Better Labor-Management Relations. The next decade may well witness a trend toward improved labor-management relations in which greater emphasis will be placed on joint problem solving. Identification of promising areas for such cooperative actions and encouragement of their use on a wider basis will be important challenges. For example, can, and should, there be a wider application of the kind of cooperative local committee approach coupled with a no-strike agreement that has recently been used in the steel industry? What are the advantages and drawbacks of productivity bargaining? Can better techniques for impasse resolution be developed? Can, or should, there be an increased role for so-called final-offer arbitration? To what extent can labor-management relations be improved by greater reliance on the assistance of professionals in this field, particularly at the state and local levels? How much scope is there for national-level "accords" between labor and management covering a wide range of economic policy issues? How desirable are such arrangements? Should additional mechanisms (and perhaps new organizations) be developed that focus on areas of common labor-management interest and concern, rather than on issues on which labor and management regard themselves as adversaries?

Reform of Retirement and Pension Policies. The nation's retirement and pension policies cover the population unevenly. There is a risk that without significant reforms in the present system, and given projected changes in inflation rates and demography, the financing of retirement could generate an intolerable burden on future working generations. Accordingly, the Committee for Economic Development is exploring these and other broad issues related to U.S. retirement policy in the coming decades, focusing on social security and other government programs as well as on private retirement and pension systems. The following are some of the issues that need to be considered: What should be the relative roles of government and private pension programs in the overall retirement system? How can adequate retirement coverage be made available to all Americans? To what extent should individuals themselves be responsible for assuring that they and their families will have a decent retirement income, and what can government do to encourage adequate individual planning in this area? What measures are necessary to assure the financial soundness of different retirement systems? How should the burden placed on retirement systems by changing demographic trends be shared among generations? To what extent (if any) should the costs associated with the expected sharp rise in the ratio of retired persons to workers after the turn of the century be reflected in higher contributions to retirement systems or modification of benefits during the next decades? To what extent can, or should, the problem be eased by increases in the retirement age and by greater emphasis on part-time work opportunities that would draw a larger number of persons into the active work force? How much should retirees be protected against the effects of inflation? What is the optimum way of providing such protection? What is the scope for improvements in vesting provisions and pension portability? How will alternative approaches to retirement policy affect saving and capital formation, and how should these effects be taken into account in formulating a national retirement policy?

Reforming U.S. Immigration Policy. The most serious aspect of the immigration problem has been the massive entry of illegal or "undocumented" workers into the United States. The total number of such workers is estimated at between 4 and 12 million. A large influx of legal and illegal aliens is likely to continue under the impact of rapidly increasing populations in Mexico and a number of other developing countries, continued severe poverty in such countries, and frequent foreign political upheavals. Failure to deal adequately with this problem and with related broader issues of immigration policy could have explosive international and domestic repercussions.

Although the inflow of foreign workers can in many cases be expected to make a constructive and necessary contribution to the U.S. economy, serious problems arise when illegal aliens come into direct competition with the more disadvantaged groups in the U.S. labor force for unskilled and low-paying jobs and when exploitation of such workers threatens to undermine present labor standards. A major challenge in this area is how to forge a rational policy based on laws and regulations that can be enforced and that involve a judicious balancing of the interests of illegal immigrants, U.S. labor, and the broader requirements of the economy.

International Economic Relations

International Trade Policy Issues. Although the Tokyo Round trade agreements and their enactment into law in 1979 were constructive steps toward better international trade relations, trade policy issues — particularly the problem of non-tariff barriers to trade — will continue to be of major importance in the 1980s. The central problem is how the system of world trade can remain orderly, equitable, and open in the face of major structural changes in international political and economic relationships that existing rules and mechanisms do not adequately take into account.

Key issues that will need to be considered include the following: How can international trading rules take better account of the numerous new forms of government intervention in the structure of domestic industry that fall under the general heading of "industrial policy"? These interventions include such measures as orderly market agreements, trigger price arrangements, and voluntary export restraints; they also encompass various forms of direct subsidies, regional assistance, and concessionary credit terms for particular industries. How can the world trading system best deal with the growing problem of trade between economies that are largely market-oriented and economies in which many major industries are owned and/or run by the government, as in Western Europe (see the next section for further discussion of this issue), or in which international trade is a government monopoly, as in the Communist Bloc countries? What rules are needed covering the safeguard arrangements that governments use to protect their economies from market disruption? To what extent should developing nations that have achieved a relatively advanced stage of industrialization (such as Brazil, Mexico, and Korea) be subjected to the entire range of GATT and other trading rules now applicable to the fully industrialized countries? Should existing international trading rules be extended to trade in services? If so, are adaptations of these trading rules needed in light of the special nature and growing importance of service transactions?

Increased Government Involvement in Business Decision Making in Foreign Countries. One special consideration cuts across virtually all the international economic relationships of the American private sector: the tendency for an enlarged share of international trade, service, and capital transactions in other countries to be conducted by government entities or by organizations under their close control. In contrast, the American counterparts of most such transactions are conducted by private organizations, with most of the key decisions being made privately (even if those decisions are sometimes constrained to some degree by law or regulation). This mismatch in the locus of decisional authority is not uniformly adverse to the U.S. interests; indeed, on average, the freer market expects to outperform bureaucratically run organizations in efficiency. But particularly in the short and intermediate terms, arrangements under which foreign governments are direct or indirect parties to a transaction can give such governments special advantages or can impose special handicaps on private-sector competition from other countries. Within the complexities of international trading, how can the importance of these mismatches be assessed? What can be done to redress them? Can fair rules of the game for government intervention be successfully incorporated in international codes of behavior? When, and in what circumstances, should such rules apply? Can their implementation be reasonably assured?

Special Issues Affecting Economic Relations among the United States, Mexico, and Canada. Over the next decade, this country's economic relations with its immediate neighbors to the north and south could prove to be a source of major friction or of significant mutual benefit. A number of specific issues will require continuing resolution, including the potential role of Mexico as a supplier of oil and gas to the United States, the degree of U.S.-Canadian energy cooperation, coping with the flows of legal and "undocumented" Mexican immigrants into the United States, and finding ways to resist pressures for undesirable restrictions on the flow of trade and investment among the three countries. More broadly, should the range of economic relations between the United States and its neighbors be approached within a more comprehensive framework, and should such an approach lead to a more formal arrangement for fuller regional economic integration?

Effects of OPEC Surpluses on Developing Countries. The rapid escalation of oil prices during 1979 and 1980 has led to a huge buildup of the current account surpluses of oil-exporting countries. According to the International Monetary Fund, the total current account surplus of these countries is estimated at about $115 billion in 1980, compared with $68 billion in 1979 and only $5 billion in 1978. Very sizable surpluses for the OPEC countries (i.e., the member nations of the Organization of Petroleum Exporting Countries) and corresponding large deficits elsewhere are likely to persist for a number of years. Although this development is likely to be a continuing source of major imbalances in the world economy generally, it poses particularly critical problems for many of the developing countries that produce little or no oil and hence must import it in quantity.

These countries may soon be unable to finance their large payment deficits by continued expansion of borrowing from private banks. Their overall foreign debt has become extremely high, and commercial banks in the United States and other developed countries are, in various cases, more inclined to retrench than to expand their lending to developing nations because they fear overexposure. (Private banks currently provide almost two-thirds of the net external financial requirements of the developing countries that are not members of OPEC, compared with less than one-third in the early 1970s.) The problem is magnified by recent tendencies on the part of the industrial nations toward slower growth and increased protectionism, making it harder for the developing countries to service their debts and pay for current needs by expanding their exports.

Should these developments lead to drastic curtailment in economic growth in many non-oil-producing developing countries, the adverse consequences both for them and for the developed nations could be profound. One result would be a major reversal of the progress toward sound economic growth that has been under way in various developing nations and a sharp concomitant increase in deprivation and political unrest. There could also be seriously adverse effects on banks and other financial institutions in the industrial countries. Moreover, severe economic retrenchment by the developing countries could exert a major negative impact on world trade and economic growth generally. Avoidance of such an outcome is likely to require a multipronged approach involving increased OPEC lending to the developing nations, enlarged financial assistance by international institutions, and sound noninflationary growth as well as basic adherence to liberal trade practices on the part of the industrial nations.

Adapting Food Policies to Changing World Supply and Demand Patterns. A critical problem in the coming decade is the urgent need for a major increase in world food production to meet the enormous expansion in the demand for food and to achieve a better balance in food output and consumption between developed and developing countries. It would be of mutual benefit to the two groups of countries if collaborative efforts were undertaken to assure that a major share of this increase will come from sharply higher food production in the developing nations. This would enable these countries to reverse their growing dependence on food imports and provide needed employment in rural areas. At the same time, it would contain the severe capacity and inflationary pressures that would be likely to result if attempts were made to meet most of the needed increase in world food output from the United

States and other developed countries. Additional issues relate to needed improvements in mechanisms for dealing with emergency food needs and the pros and cons of creating an international grain reserve.

Population Pressures in Developing Countries. Beyond the special issue of food, there looms the more general problem posed by the pressure that growing populations in a number of developing countries place on their limited physical and financial resources. Although the gross national output of most of these countries is growing, this advance is in a number of cases being challenged or even seriously outstripped by the pace of population growth. As a result, the rise in the already meager per capita living standards in these cases is being held down or even reversed, particularly outside the most industrialized areas in these countries. Powerful local forces, including national pride, social traditions, and inadequate education, are important contributors to this dilemma. The question facing developed countries is what they can, and should, properly do to assist developing countries in its resolution. The issue is not only a matter of simple humanity but also one of long-run viability of the world's production growth and distribution patterns.

Supporting Services

Growth and Use of New Information Technologies. The 1980s are likely to witness a further information explosion. According to one recent study, over half of all U.S. jobs will shortly be centered in information-related activities. Rapid advances in computer technology, cable television, electronic mail, microfilming techniques, and numerous other innovations will give people instant access to an extraordinary wealth of information in their offices and their homes. Key issues will be how this information system can best be coordinated and utilized to be of greatest benefit to society and what can be done to optimize the quality of information as well as the cost effectiveness of its delivery.

Better Relationships between the Media and Other Key Institutions. Improvements in national policies are vitally dependent on better public understanding of relevant issues. Such understanding, in turn, is strongly influenced by what is reported in the media. Particularly in the economic field, however, newspaper reporters and analysts frequently lack a basic understanding of underlying concepts and issues and of the role of key institutions, especially the business sector. A major task for the 1980s will be to develop better channels of communication and a more constructive dialogue between the media and the business sector and to place much greater emphasis on improving the general economic education of the press.

Adapting Education to Changing Needs and Trends. Education, one of the biggest sectors of activity in America, is already under considerable pressure because of its deteriorating performance relative to expectations. This appears to result in part from laggard and misguided responses of the educational bureaucracy to changing environments and student needs. Such pressures seem likely to continue in the years ahead, with declining populations in the traditional student age range in many areas of the country, increasing proportions of relatively disadvantaged young people, resurgent pressures on schools to gear curricula more directly to income-earning activities, and an exploding rate of increase in overall information. How much can the relative decline in the teen-age student population usefully be offset by expanding adult education? Can schools develop effective multitrack curricula, imparting vocational or professional skills as well as providing cultural enrichment to widely differing age groups and proficiency levels? Can vocational education be made more directly relevant to jobs so that the school-to-work transition will be less painful than it is at present? Is more specialized and job-specific education in fact a worthwhile goal? Are there ways for schools to do a better job of narrowing gaps in knowledge, particularly at primary-skill levels, thereby promoting more equality of opportunity? Rapidly rising education costs underline the importance of a final question: How can technology, learning psychology, organizational management, and other sciences be utilized to make education much more cost-effective than it is today?

Reforming the Welfare System. Although public interest in welfare reform has somewhat receded recently, the issue will continue to be of major importance in the coming decade. A central question is whether a federally supported program can, and should, be established within a reasonable fiscal framework that would provide adequate minimum income levels for all those in need but that would, at the same time, include sufficient work and training incentives and requirements for those who are able to work.

The following are some of the specific issues that need to be resolved: Should minimum national levels of income be established under such a federally supported program? If so, what should they be? Should such benefits be available to the working poor as well as to those who do not work? To what extent should the federal government assume responsibility for the financing and/or administration of public welfare programs? Should such federal responsibility be significantly increased, or on the contrary, should the responsibility be largely or entirely entrusted to the states? How can the overall design and administration of the welfare system be changed to make it both more equitable and more efficient? Can, and should, various types of public assistance programs, including food stamps, housing assistance, and medical benefits, be brought into an integrated system? What can be done to improve work incentives under welfare programs so that a larger part of the welfare population will be able to escape the morass of permanent welfare dependency? How can individuals on welfare be offered more adequate job and training opportunities, particularly in the private sector?

Meeting Growing Demands for Health Care in More Cost-Effective Ways. American medical science has made great advances in curing disease, easing human distress, and prolonging life. But these advances have been accompanied by great increases in the nation's total bill for health care. A number of factors have contributed to this situation. Many newer medical advances involve expensive training, treatment, and capital equipment. The interrelated phenomena of a growing proportion of aged persons in the population, the prolonged life of the average individual, and the longer exposure of individuals to the costly-to-treat illnesses of later life all combine to increase health care expenses. Greatly expanded health insurance coverage through the growth of private prepaid insurance plans and such public programs as Medicare and Medicaid has contributed to a major expansion in the effective demand for health services. This, in turn, has exerted strong pressures on the supply and price of available health care resources in various parts of the country. The increased availability of third-party payments for medical care has tended to make cost control more difficult. Finally, the same overall inflationary forces that push up prices in general have added their impetus to the rise in cost of health care.

What are the most promising approaches for increasing cost effectiveness and reducing inflationary pressures in the health care field? How can better incentives and disincentives (affecting suppliers as well as users of health care) be built into the system to reduce upward pressures on costs? To what extent can this objective be achieved by relatively greater emphasis on prevention of illnesses and out-of-hospital services rather than in-hospital care that may not be needed? How can programs to provide more adequate health care coverage for the population and to give families and individuals protection against excessive financial burdens as a result of needed medical care be developed in a way that will contain rather than exacerbate the inflation of health care costs?

Better Care for the Increasing Number of Aged Persons. With the continuing expansion in the size of the aged population and the simultaneous enormous rise in the cost of nursing homes and other institutional care for older people, increasing attention will have to be devoted to more humane, dignified, and cost-effective ways of coping with the problems of the aged. Many of the aged can lead useful and productive lives outside of institutions if they can avoid isolation, neglect, and depression. A major challenge will be to gear transportation systems, safety measures, and other urban facilities more fully and sensitively to the requirements of older people. At the same time, expanded and more effective ways will have to be found to provide adequate special care to many older people in their own homes and to allow them to participate in constructive community activities rather than consign them to institutions.

Strengthening the Social Service Role of Private Nonprofit Organizations. A special feature of American society has been the humanitarian role played by private volunteer efforts and nonprofit organizations. The kinds of growing social needs exemplified by the problems of the aging population and extending to many other groups in our society can be expected to call for substantially increased and more effective use of nonprofit organizations and private volunteer efforts. However, various recent developments, including less favorable tax treatment and administrative rules as well as lagging contributions, are raising serious questions about the future ability of nonprofit organizations to continue even their present scale of operations. What can be done to strengthen the ability of the nonprofit sector to respond effectively to the social needs of the 1980s?

Adapting the Transportation System to a Changing Environment. Our capital-intensive transportation system represents one of the largest investments in the economy. It is under powerful pressures for very substantial change, partly for demographic reasons, partly for technological reasons, but most importantly because of the huge increase in the cost of petroleum, its chief source of motive power. This combination of pressures has raised important strategic questions concerning future policies affecting the intercity and intracity transportation of individuals and goods and services. Such pressures are likely to have implications for the future residential patterns and the location of facilities for the production of goods and services.

For example, what implications will the high cost of energy over the foreseeable future have for the development of public rail and road transportation to facilitate the movement of individuals to and from work and cultural activities? What does it imply for the relative reliance placed on the use of private automobiles and mass transit? What implications will this have for residential development within metropolitan areas and for the location of industry and services in urban areas? To what extent will it be possible to substitute telecommunications for transportation? More generally, how can the need for transportation be reduced by bringing work closer to where people live?

Inasmuch as railroads now appear to be the most energy-efficient form of transportation for many goods, would it be wise to increase reliance on rail services? Can the basic rail network be upgraded sufficiently to provide reliable expanded service? What are the implications for air and highway transportation, with their hitherto attractive advantages of speed and convenience? Can technological advances reduce the relative burden of energy costs enough to preserve their role as preeminent carriers?

Because transportation costs are likely to constitute an increasing proportion of costs of production and household budget expenditures, to what extent should there be private-public cooperation in the development of a more integrated transportation system within which each form of transportation will contribute to minimizing transportation costs for commuting and providing goods for the market?

In many industries, adjustments of this sort are handled predominantly by the market system. For a variety of reasons, however, decision making in the transportation industry has been a tangle of public and private rules, practices, and bureaucratic procedures that slows adaptation. To what extent will reformed decision-making structures be needed to reach the strategic decisions that will reshape the transportation system?

ABOUT THE AUTHOR

FRANK W. SCHIFF has been Vice President and Chief Economist of the Committee for Economic Development (CED) since April 1969. He previously served as Deputy Undersecretary of the Treasury for Monetary Affairs (1968–1969); Senior Staff Economist, President's Council of Economic Advisers (1964–1968); research economist and officer of the Federal Reserve Bank of New York (1951–1964); and on the economics faculty of Columbia University (1946–1951), where he also received his undergraduate and graduate training in economics. At CED, he has been project director for numerous policy statements on a wide range of issues, including *Fighting Inflation and Rebuilding a Sound Economy* (1980), *Helping Insure Our Energy Future: A Program for Developing Synthetic Fuel Plants Now* (1979), *Jobs for the Hard-to-Employ: New Directions for a Public-Private Partnership* (1978), and earlier studies *High Employment Without Inflation: A Positive Program for Economic Stabilization* and *Strengthening the World Monetary System*. He is past president and chairman of the National Economists Club and a member of the Council on Foreign Relations, has been active on the Atlantic Council's Working Group dealing with coordination of international economic policies, and serves as an adviser to the Bureau of Labor Statistics, the Rockefeller Foundation, the Work in America Institute, and the National Council for Alternative Work Patterns.